S. Wesley Ariarajah

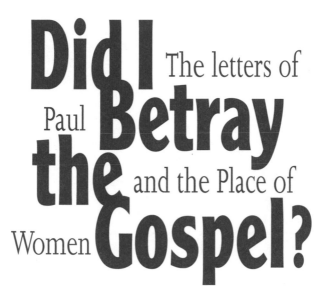

Did I The letters of
Paul **Betray**
the and the Place of
Women **Gospel?**

KT-377-820

Risk
BOOK SERIES

WCC Publications, Geneva

Second printing August 1996

Cover design: Edwin Hassink/WCC

ISBN 2-8254-1183-3

© 1996 WCC Publications, World Council of Churches,
150 route de Ferney, 1211 Geneva 2, Switzerland

Risk Book Series No. 70

Printed in Switzerland

Table of Contents

Did I Betray the Gospel?

To our daughters

Dharshi, Niro and Anu

Prologue

How This Book Came To Be Written

There is a story behind this book.

The World Council of Churches has been active on the issue of justice for women in church and society from its very beginnings. Its founding assembly (Amsterdam 1948) set up a permanent commission on the life and work of women in the church.

Following the second assembly in 1954, the Department on the Co-operation of Men and Women in Church and Society was created, with ecumenical pioneer Madeleine Barot as its first executive secretary. Later this became the sub-unit on Women in Church and Society.

The task of the "Women's Desk", as it was often referred to, was both advocacy for women and mobilizing them around the issues that concerned them. A major conference on "Sexism in the 1970s", held in Berlin in 1974, helped to put these issues firmly on the agenda of the churches.

Following the WCC's fifth assembly in Nairobi in 1975, a worldwide study process on the "Community of Women and Men in the Church" was established in the Faith and Order Commission to animate theological discussions on the place and role of women specifically within the churches. This study opened up discussion in the churches on such difficult issues as biblical interpretation, tradition, sexuality and ministry. The work of many local study groups was brought together in a world conference in 1981 in Sheffield, England.

Over these decades massive changes have also taken place in society, resulting in significant shifts in women's self-understanding, their roles in society and the relationship between women and men.

Perhaps the most important instruments of change have been the movements among women themselves. The women's movements have helped to examine and challenge some of the basic assumptions on which traditional self-understandings, relationships and structures have been built.

Declaration of a Decade

In 1987 the WCC declared that the ten years from 1988 to 1998 should be marked as an Ecumenical Decade of

Churches in Solidarity with Women, to focus attention more sharply on these issues and to help churches to examine their own life in terms of their commitment to justice for women. This declaration was timely. It was time to take stock, to discern where we are today on this issue.

But what use have churches made of the Decade? What are some of the key issues emerging? In order to assess this and to encourage and enable the churches in their effort, the WCC decided to send teams of persons to all its member churches at the midpoint of the Decade. The teams have been listening to the churches, raising questions that help in the assessment and meeting with relevant groups.

I myself went on a mid-Decade team visit to Pakistan, a visit that took our team to all the major cities of Pakistan, beginning in Karachi to the Afghan border in the north.

The influence of biblical teaching

Much could be said about the situation of women around the world on the basis of these visits. But one of the key issues that emerged almost everywhere was that of the biblical teaching on the place of women in the church and their relationship to men, especially in the context of the family.

Most Christians, notably of the Protestant tradition, are what I have come to call "Bible Christians". What they believe has to be biblical. In itself this is a wonderful thing. For where else can we draw the basis and the primary inspiration for our faith but the Bible? Many of these Christians arrive at the "biblical faith" or "biblical teaching" by way of a special process. It begins with a general, strong and uncritical affirmation that "the Bible is the word of God" and what is taught by the Bible is what we should believe in.

Some in this group are willing to go behind the biblical texts to understand them in context. But most settle down to accepting literally whatever is written. Any effort to place the texts in context is seen as an attempt to distort biblical teaching.

In several mid-Decade visits team members encountered situations in which the place accorded to women in the church, society and the family was defended with biblical texts, drawn especially from the letters of St Paul.

There are of course some who use Paul to justify what they believe in any case. But there are others who are genuinely puzzled. Since they begin with the belief that the Bible, as it is written, is the Word of God, they have considerable difficulty in knowing what to do with such clear statements by Paul as "Women should keep silence in the church", "I permit no women to speak", "Women were made for men", "Wives, obey your husbands".

Most of these people are aware of the radical changes that have been going on in the understanding of the place of women in church and society, but they cannot relate this to what appears to be a clear teaching on this matter by St Paul. To them the question simply becomes: "Are we to say that the Bible is wrong on this matter? If so, how can we believe that the Bible is the word of God?"

A book on women and St Paul

In this context some colleagues approached me with a request to write a book on this matter along the lines of my earlier book, *The Bible and People of Other Faiths*, in which I tried to interpret the biblical teaching for the emerging new relationship between Christians and peoples of other religious traditions. That book, like this one, was directed to members of congregations.

Having accepted the task, the first thing I did was to read again all the letters of Paul, each letter at one stretch. My fears were confirmed! One of my colleagues had already warned me that "on this one matter, St Paul cannot be redeemed". For a moment I was tempted to believe him.

My own attitude to the Pauline epistles has been rather mixed. In my earlier book I have complained about Paul's preoccupation with proving that Jesus was the promised Messiah and his apparent lack of interest in what Jesus had taught, which made him inaccessible to people of other faiths.

It is no secret that Paul was quarrelsome and argumentative. His co-workers at times abandoned him because of deep disagreements with him. Always bent on proving his point, he never spared his opponents.

But Paul also had a firm grasp of the gospel and was completely immersed in the grace, love, freedom and joy that came with his encounter with Christ. His commitment to his mission was total. He remains the first Christian mystic.

For these reasons, I have studied Paul closely and I know several Pauline passages by heart. And yet he presented many difficulties, including what he had to say on women.

I did not know quite how to deal with the task assigned to me. Then early one morning it dawned on me that St Paul is perhaps the one personality in the Bible who needs no one else to defend him. He was so much under attack in his ministry that much of what he wrote in his letters consists of a defence of his apostleship and the gospel he preached.

Why not ask Paul himself to give advice on issues that have been raised in the course of the team visits on the place of women in church and society? If he were here today, in our own times, what would he say about what he himself had written about women some 2000 years ago? What advice might he give on some of the issues raised in our visits, including that of women in the ministry?

New letters by St Paul

I have, therefore, written four imaginary letters by St Paul. The first letter, addressed to all Christians, takes up the main passages in Paul's letters that deal with women. "How are we to understand them today?", I asked of the contemporary St Paul.

The second takes the form of a letter of advice to a Reverend Daniel, who has asked Paul's guidance on the deep divisions that have surfaced in his congregation over the issue of the ordination of women.

The third, in the form of a second letter addressed to all Christians, is along the lines of 1 Corinthians, where Paul writes to the church on issues and matters in the congregation that have been referred to him for advice. Here I have included some of the specific issues that have stood out in the mid-Decade team visits.

The fourth letter is addressed to a Christian named Marcus, who has difficulty in dealing with contemporary questions raised about women's participation because they contradict the scripture which he and his congregation believe to be the word of God. In what sense is the Bible the word of God? How do we discern God's will today from what was written 2000 years ago in a different culture and in a different historical setting? I thought it would be good to ask Paul to address this issue as well.

Paul, a man of his times

It is very important to realize that Paul was a man of his times. He lived in a patriarchal society where man was accepted as the head of the household. Most of the leadership in public life at that time was exercised by men.

In his letters Paul does not challenge this basic social structure. In fact the whole concept of equality of women and men, *as we know and advocate today*, was not an issue for him. None of his letters has sections specifically concerned with justice for women as we understand this today. On the contrary, Paul often comes across as someone who has uncritically accepted the social order of his time.

In this sense it is futile to attempt to prove that Paul had views on women and the family that would satisfy us today. In fact, considering the times in which he lived, it is unreasonable to expect this of him.

For this reason I decided that the only way to deal with the issue was to ask: "As someone who had come under the influence of the gospel, what would Paul say if he were to write letters to congregations in our own times?"

Therefore I ask of Pauline scholars to bear with me when the interpretations of his thoughts do go beyond what he had intended in his original letters. And if some readers think that I have defended Paul too much, remember that we are dealing with the Paul of today, and not of yesterday.

That is why new letters had to be written.

Is this a legitimate exercise?

I have had considerable reservations about doing what I have done. St Paul's letters are held in such high regard as part of the Christian scripture that it might seem, at least to some, to be disrespectful of Paul and of the scriptures to write letters in Paul's name.

What is more, it would indeed be a curious and unwelcome practice if people were to decide to put forward their own peculiar ideas in the names of Paul and Peter and so on.

Therefore I decided to set some limits. The specific self-discipline I imposed in writing these letters was that everything said must arise from what I believe to be Paul's own grasp and understanding of the gospel in his original letters.

In other words, these letters were controlled by this one question: "If Paul were to live in the changed situation of today, what would he say in respect to the place and role of women in church and society, based on the understanding of the gospel and of the Christian faith which we find in his own epistles?"

Paul was a very learned man. Pauline epistles are very rich in vocabulary, style and form. It is very difficult to imitate him. I have tried as far as possible to stay close to Paul's style in his original letters and his argumentative method of putting the issues forward. I have also purposely stayed close to his theological positions in his epistles to draw his new arguments.

Whether I have succeeded in staying close to Paul's own theology and in interpreting him for today, only the reader can judge. From those who think I have failed — and from those who in any case are uneasy about the whole idea of writing letters in Paul's name — I ask forbearance.

S. Wesley Ariarajah

1. Did I Betray the Gospel?

A Letter to the Christians

Greetings

1 Grace to you and peace from our Lord Jesus Christ, through whom God has called us to a glorious and imperishable hope. I am amazed at all times by the wonderful and mysterious ways of God. By the power of the Holy Spirit, the message of the gospel has indeed been taken to the very ends of the earth.

I rejoice in the thought that the name of Christ is known in every continent, and that in every nation there are faithful hearts that invoke the name of Christ for God's own praise and glory.

How rich and unfathomable are God's ways! How dependable are God's promises!

I raise my heart in ceaseless thanksgiving, knowing that I and all others who laboured for the gospel did not run our race in vain, but that God who began the good work in us is bringing it to its perfection.

Quarrels over my letters

I am dismayed to hear that the letters I wrote to churches and individuals, which have now become the common property of all of you Christians, have become the subject of deep dissension among you, especially in understanding the place and role of women in the church and in the family.

It grieves me beyond measure to know that what I wrote to settle quarrels within specific churches and to guide them in seeking peaceable solutions has itself become the basis of division and enmity among you.

The purpose of my letters

In all the letters I wrote to different churches in Asia Minor, Rome and other places where, by God's grace, I was given the task of establishing Christian communities, I had no intention other than to strengthen the life of the Christian people.

I wrote to help them in their struggle with the problems they faced as new Christians in a complex world, and to guide them as far as I was able on the questions which they themselves first raised with me on matters of faith and Christian life.

God is my witness as to how I agonized over some of those questions. And those who lived with me know that I spent sleepless nights in my attempt to give counsel regarding matters on which I myself was still seeking guidance and on which we had no word from the Lord.

But did I write back to those congregations and say that I had no advice to give? Did I say that my task was over when the gospel was preached, and that as Christians they were now expected to find their own individual answers?

Did I refrain from giving advice for fear that what I said on the basis of my own wisdom might be challenged or changed when the Spirit led the churches into new ways of being obedient to the gospel?

God forbid! How could I abandon those congregations which were God's own gifts of grace to the ministry that was entrusted to me? And I knew how grateful they were to me that I had brought the glorious gospel of liberation to them; how much they loved me and supported me in my ministry in other parts of Asia Minor.

While I suffered in my bonds I had heard from my beloved son Timothy of how my friends in these churches prayed ceaselessly for my well-being, sometimes through the whole night, with hands lifted high and with tears in their eyes. I know how they longed for me to be released from my chains so that they might see me again in the flesh.

No, I had no choice but to write back to them and guide them as far as I could: sometimes reminding them of the commandments of the Lord; sometimes prompting them to let the freedom they had gained in the gospel guide them in their decisions; often advising them to put love above all things, knowing that what comes out of love is what the Lord requires of us.

I was also not ashamed to admit that on many matters I had no word from the Lord. On those issues I gave my own opinion, shaped as it might have been by my own upbringing and the times in which I lived.

I took the risk of giving guidance on so many matters because the Lord who searches our hearts knows that in everything I did, and in every advice I gave, I had no other purpose than the upbuilding of the church.

In all these, was I true to the gospel? Was I faithful to my calling as an apostle? Let the Lord be my judge.

Anger among the sisters

I hear that some of the sisters among you reject me and my letters totally, saying, "Paul is no help to us in our understanding of the gospel as women!"

And I know that others of you are angry with me to the point of accusing me of robbing you of the freedom God granted you in Christ Jesus.

Woe to me if I rob anyone of you of the glorious freedom, equality and justice that is yours in the gospel! Would I not be distorting the gospel, and stand condemned in the sight of God, if I taught that there was one gospel for men and another for women? Is it at all possible that the same gospel which brings freedom to the one should become the bondage of another?

I would be the least of all apostles if the message I shared with you resulted in some of you having to carry more burdens than the others.

Am I a betrayer of the gospel?

Do not jump to hasty conclusions

How then could you be so easily persuaded that the sermons I preached and the letters I wrote require women to be subordinated to men for all times?

You are foolish to take the advice I gave in a specific situation so as to bring order into the life of one congregation in a given culture, and use it to discriminate against women of your day.

For I was speaking as a person from a given culture to a people living at a specific period of history. Or did you think that I was an angel coming down from heaven, untouched by human frailty?

Am I not a man? Am I not of the Jewish culture, a Hebrew born of Hebrews? Was I not giving advice to Christians under persecution who could easily have been put to the sword for bringing disgrace on the prevalent understandings that shaped family life?

You are aware, sisters and brothers, that I wrote in my second letter to the Corinthians that now that we know Christ in the spirit, we no longer know anyone from a human point of view, and that if anyone — and I repeat, *anyone*, male or female — is in Christ there is a new creation; that the old has passed away and everything has become new (2 Cor. 5:16f.).

Have you forgotten how forcefully I argued with the church in Galatia, plagued as it was by so many false teachers who were ready to lead them back into bondage, that in Christ there is neither Jew nor Greek, slave nor free, male nor female (Gal. 3:28)?

Am I a hypocrite?

What then can we say? Am I a hypocrite? Do I preach freedom in one place and bondage in another? Would I have been ready to risk my life at the hands of ungodly men for the sake of a gospel that was only partially true, or true only for some and not for others — depending on their race, caste or gender? By no means!

My beloved brothers and sisters, by the grace that is given to me, let me assure you that there is only one gospel that frees us all, men and women, and makes us precious and equal in the sight of God.

If we are equal before God, it goes without saying that we are also equal before one another. How can what is precious in God's eyes become worthless in our eyes?

We must not pretend to be wiser than God. Is God's justice so twisted as to say to a man, "You are my child", and something else to a woman for whom Christ also suffered the cross? Did Christ die for some and not for all?

Perhaps I am wearing you out with all my questions. But what else can I do if you have so easily and so quickly moved away from the central message I preached, for which I was prepared to face insult and injury, imprisonment and death?

What I have said to you before, I say to you again: In Christ there is neither male nor female; if anyone is in Christ there is a new creation; the old has passed away and the new has come.

Cover your heads

2 I have been told that several among you are deeply disappointed with me for what I wrote in my first letter to the church in Corinth requiring that women should cover their heads (1 Cor. 11:2-16). "It is not just the covering of the head," one of you has said, "but also that you have argued that the man is 'the image and reflection of God; but woman is the reflection of man' (v.7). And to buttress the argument you also say that 'man was not made from woman, but woman from man'"(v.8).

"Is this the freedom in Christ you are talking about? Does this passage not teach that women are completely subordinate to men and that the only purpose of their existence is to reflect the glory of men and to be used by them? Are you aware that in many churches these words of yours are used to deny the freedom God has given to us as women?"

Sisters and brothers, first let me say that if any man uses what I have written to argue that the scriptures require men to dominate women, he is using scripture to satisfy and justify his own selfish wishes and desires. Do not believe him. If I had said, "Let all men be subjected to women and see them as their glory", would he have said, "Let us men be subjected to women for Paul has said so"? Would he say, "This is scripture; let us subject ourselves to it"? Indeed not!

Let us not be deceived by those who twist and turn scripture and use selected portions of it to maintain what their unrepentant hearts desire most. If the preaching of the gospel leads some of us to become subordinated to others, we are to be pitied among all people; and the gospel we have preached is not one of liberation but one that brings servitude.

For if you continue to read that passage, you will note that, having given the traditional understanding of the relationship of women and men, I go on to say how it is to be perceived "in the Lord". "Nevertheless," I have argued, "in the Lord woman is not independent of man or man independent of woman. For just as woman came from man, so man comes through woman; but all things come from God" (vv.11-12).

By using the word "nevertheless", I contrast the freedom that we have "in the Lord" with how the man-woman relationship was structured within the traditions of the society.

It is in the strength of the freedom we have in the gospel that I could tell those men, who thought that they were accountable to no one, that man is not independent of woman. And since the tradition taught that the woman is subordinate to the man "because she came out of his side", I had to remind the men that they had themselves come out of the wombs of women.

The context of the letter

Sisters and brothers, I do not want you to be ignorant of the circumstances under which I wrote this first letter to the Corinthians.

You will recall that when I went from Athens to Corinth for the first time, I found Aquila and Priscilla, who had only recently arrived there after the emperor Claudius ordered all Jews to leave Rome (Acts 18:1-18).

It was as if the Lord had hardened the heart of Claudius so that I might have the good company and generous hospitality of these two, who became my lifelong co-workers and friends. Since they too were tent-makers, I stayed and worked with them for eighteen months.

When I came to Corinth it was not my intention to preach the gospel to the Gentiles, but only to proclaim in the synagogue that Jesus was the Messiah promised by the prophets.

Although I found some followers among the Jews, I met with strong opposition from my own people. I was even dragged to the tribunal of Gallio, the proconsul of Achaia, and charged with teaching people to live in ways contrary to the Jewish law.

And when Gallio refused to take up the case because it had to do with the internal life of the Jewish community, they released all the anger they had towards me on Sosthenes, an official of the synagogue who had become a Christian. They beat him up right in front of the tribunal; and Gallio paid no attention to it.

Turning to the Gentiles

So I turned to the Gentiles. But what a group they were! You are perhaps aware that Corinth was the capital of the Roman province of Achaia, a thriving commercial city in which people from many nations lived. They came from all parts of the Roman empire and brought with them all the vices of the empire.

At the centre of the city stood the temple of Aphrodite, with a thousand priestess-prostitutes attached to it. And the city was rife with all manner of sects, religious cults and mystery religions which taught self-gratification and sexual exploits as ways to spiritual liberation.

Women were being enticed from the bonds of the family into believing that selling their bodies to ritual prostitution would bring both self-fulfilment and spiritual release.

My first thought was to leave the vile city, but the Lord himself appeared to me in a dream to convince me that I should stay there despite my reservations about the devastating culture of the place (Acts 18:9).

The proclamation of the gospel bore fruit, and many Corinthians became believers and were baptized (v.8).

Problems in the Corinthian church

It was years later, when the church in Corinth sent me a letter raising numerous issues on which divisions and dissensions had arisen, that I realized how much the local culture was threatening the life of the Christian community. In fact, they listed the problems one by one and asked for detailed guidance on each.

I wish you had seen that letter. How anguished they were, watched on the one hand by the Jews, who opposed them and were ever ready to challenge their way of life and the truth of their allegiance to the Lord, and pressed on the other hand by the local culture to exercise their freedom to live in any way that pleased them.

Did the freedom they had in Christ, whether as Jews or as Gentiles, entitle them to live as they pleased? Were there no laws to govern the conduct and behaviour of those who had become Christians? Were they freed from all responsibilities as husbands and wives to each other and to their children? Is the gospel message about disorder and chaos? God forbid!

I entreat you, brothers and sisters, to read the whole of my first letter to the Corinthians, in one sitting if you can, in order to become more aware of its purpose and directions.

There were several problems in the life of the church in Corinth that I had heard about (chs 1-6): divisions within the church, adherence to mystery cults, sexual immorality, taking other Christians to courts.

On several other questions they had written to ask my advice: problems related to marriage and remaining single, to the situation in which a person becomes a Christian while his or her partner remains in another faith, to eating meat offered to idols, to the proper way of celebrating the Lord's supper, to the primacy of spiritual gifts.

Women and freedom in the gospel

It is in this context that they also asked me about women who wished to exercise their freedom by shaving their heads or refusing to cover them at times of worship. Some were even claiming that as freed persons they were not bound to their husbands but might take to themselves anyone they liked.

Was this the freedom of the gospel that I had preached to them? In Corinth it was only the prostitutes of the temple of Aphrodite who shaved their heads as a mark of devotion to the goddess of fertility. And it was the women of the spirit cults who let their unbound hair fall all around them as they sang and danced around the altar.

If the Jews of Corinth were to see the unbound hair of a Christian woman, would they not think that she had been caught in adultery?

I could not agree that the freedom Christ has offered in the gospel be witnessed to in such hideous ways. The gospel of Christ is too precious to be belittled, and I did not want to give the opponents of the church in Corinth any room to spread the story that women who became Christian entered prostitution or were free to become adulterous.

The gospel of Christ is not about chaos and disorder but about love and unity. Therefore I had to insist that they should not shave their heads and must cover them during worship.

The power of discernment

Concerning the covering of the head, I am disappointed to learn that there are men and even women among you who argue that women in every part of the world should cover their heads in church because I ordained that it should be so in Corinth.

Where is your power of discernment? Are you not aware that it was a general practice of the time that women covered their head as an expression of their womanhood and as a mark of respect in a place of worship? In no way was I introducing a new law.

You know that there are different ways in which communities mark their respect for a place of worship. Some remove their shoes, some put on special clothing, some cover their heads.

If the women of a place always covered their head in worship as a sign of their womanhood and out of respect for God, could I exempt those women who had become Christians from this practice?

And where it is the practice for men not to cover their head in places of worship, would I tolerate those men who want to make a show of their so-called freedom by covering their heads?

No, I insist that the freedom we have in Christ is not to be trivialized. If covering the head is the way one honours God in a culture, let the Christians of that culture also do so. We cannot be counted among those who dishonour God or disrespect a place of worship.

For the same reason, if in another culture it is not the normal practice for women to cover their heads as a mark of respect, is it not foolish to insist that they do so? What purpose does it serve?

Do you not see that the question is not about covering or uncovering heads but about honouring and dishonouring God?

Church is not a place for showing off

For this same reason I had to say some harsh words in my first letter to Timothy (2:8-10) concerning both men and women who were part of his fellowship.

Some of the men were using the occasion of gathering for worship as the time to settle their quarrels and arguments. And some of the women among them used the occasion to braid their hair in unusual fashions and to don themselves with gold, pearls and expensive clothes to impress others with their wealth and importance (vv.8-9).

Is worship the time for men to show their anger to each other? Is the time of prayer intended for women to show off their wealth and fashions? I had to admonish both groups, calling on the men to stop their arguments and raise their hands to heaven in holy praise, and appealing to the women to dress modestly in a manner suitable for the occasion.

In all these things I desired nothing more than that God, who has called us to a living hope in Christ, be praised and glorified in all our worship, and that our Christian life and behaviour, whether we are men or women, not be a scandal to the gospel.

Are women inferior to men?

3 Now concerning the equality of women and men, I am aware that what I have written in several places in my letters to the churches and to my beloved child in the faith Timothy has caused considerable anguish among you, my sisters.

I am aware that several leaders and teachers of the faith among you, including many men, understand what I have written on matters of family relationships as reflecting what was accepted within a specific culture at that particular time.

But I am also told that others among you insist that what I have set forth in my writings should be the nature of the relationship between husband and wife for all times.

I would be pleased to be taken so seriously if those same men were also saying to each other, "Let us truly love our wives and honour them, because Paul has instructed us to do so"; or if all of you were saying to one another, "Let us put away our differences and come together around the Lord's table because Paul has taught us that 'there is only one Lord, one faith and one baptism' and that we must at all times strive to 'preserve the unity of the spirit in the bond of peace'."

Be that as it may, let me not run away from dealing with the charge that in some of my letters I have urged the subordination of women to men and argued that such subordination is warranted by scripture (Eph. 5:21-24; 1 Cor. 11:8; 1 Tim. 2:13).

In all honesty, let me tell you that this is what I was taught, and this was the generally accepted basis on which family relationships were built in the society in which I lived.

Given the realities of society at that time, the love and care of the husband for his wife, the submission and respect of the wife towards her husband, the obedience of children to their parents and the willingness of everyone to live under God's law were laid down as the prerequisites for the stability of the family and the nation. And all of this, as was customary in the teaching of the rabbis, was argued on the basis of the scripture.

Of the two stories of creation in the book of Genesis, the second one, in which Eve was created out of the side of Adam, was interpreted by some teachers to emphasize that the woman was created after the man to be his help and companion. And the woman was presented as the weaker sex because it was she who succumbed to the serpent's temptation.

But you are aware that according to the first story of creation God created Adam — meaning "humankind" in Hebrew — from the very beginning as male and female: "Male and female he created them" (Gen. 1:26f.). If the second story points to subordination, does this first one not argue for equality of women and men in the sight of God and of each other?

Again, even in the second account, could not the words, "It is not good that the man should be alone", and Adam's own proclamation, "This at last is bone of my bone and flesh of my flesh" (Gen. 2:18,33), be interpreted as a call for oneness and mutuality, rather than for subordination of the one to the other?

If Eve was weak to allow herself to be tempted by the serpent, how is it that Adam is not weak in allowing himself to be tempted by Eve?

If from the beginning women had been the interpreters of the scriptures, would the choice of the story between the two accounts and the lines of interpretation not have been different?

A new argument?

Some will no doubt say that now I am suddenly playing a new tune. Am I trying to cover up what I have written before by confusing you with another set of scriptures and another set of interpretations? But I do not deceive myself into thinking that if I say something different now, I can deny what I have said before or escape the disappointment you have expressed.

All I want to say is that while the interpretation of the very same scriptures could easily have established a different model for understanding family relationships, the one which prevailed at that time was a hierarchical model, beginning with God, then men, women and children.

And when people move away from the disciplines of these relationships, it is our normal practice to quote the scripture and interpretation that were used to order the relationships in the first place.

So when I appealed to the scripture to entreat wives to submit to their husbands, or for husbands to love their wives, I was doing no more than reminding them of the framework within which their relationships had already been established in the community and the society at that time.

I was not drawing out of the scripture a new argument that women should listen to their husbands. I was only recalling the rabbinic arguments given for the practice.

What mattered in rabbinic teaching was not the soundness of the argument but the practice that results from it. It is not uncommon in my tradition to find biblical arguments to confirm practices that were already believed to foster life in family and community.

Stretching the scriptural text to the breaking point and squeezing out the last drop of possible argument are quite admissible in the rabbinic tradition.

This is allowed because no interpretation is understood to be the final or only possible interpretation of a biblical passage. For if the meaning of any passage could be interpreted by one person once and for all, then Torah would not be the living Word. No, in the rabbinic understanding, scripture must be interpreted again and again and yet again, and in a hundred different ways, so that it will speak to every generation. There can be no end to the meanings and practices that might be drawn from it.

This is the tradition from which I come.

Reasonable disciplines

Therefore, my brothers and sisters, do not think that I have set forth or reinstated for you the one and only possible interpretation of the story of Adam and Eve and the pattern of man-woman relationship that it demands.

By no means! To claim so would be to blaspheme, for no human being is allowed to claim that he or she has uncovered for all time the unfathomable mysteries of the Torah and the practices that should follow from it.

So let us, as mature men and women, get this issue into some reasonable proportion. Did I teach that a woman should submit to her husband? Yes, I did. And did I use one of the streams of rabbinic interpretation of the creation story to sustain my argument? Of course.

Did I believe that the husband was the head of the family, in which love and care on the part of the husband, submission and respect on the part of the wife and obedience on the part of the children were the cornerstones of family life? Yes, indeed. I have no reason to hide the convictions that stood behind my letters.

I was convinced, as were most teachers of my time, that these were reasonable disciplines required of the different partners in the family, which corresponded to the roles assigned to different partners in the economic and the social environment in which families lived.

The words "submit" and "obey", even if they were abused by men, did not mean, as every Hebrew family knows, slavery for women, nor that women had no say in matters of family life. Far from it. It was counterbalanced by the requirement that the husband should "love" and "honour" his wife.

Was I harsh and insistent in some of my letters on the demands and obligations which husbands and wives have towards one another? Indeed I was, for I was not willing to condone the claims being made by some that becoming a Christian released them from their family obligations.

If the preaching of the gospel led to the breakdown of the family, if women were set aside with no one to support them, if men and women felt so free that they were no longer faithful to one another, what would I have gained for the gospel? Would they not have been better off without the gospel?

Pastoral guidance

For this reason, as I said before, I was deeply agitated when I heard that some of the women in Corinth not only wanted to shave their heads or let their hair hang loose like ones caught in adultery, but also wanted to claim the freedom of the gospel as freedom from their husbands. I insisted with them, using every argument available to me from scripture, that they stay within the disciplines of family life which were designed to hold families together (1 Cor. 11:1-16).

When, in this instance, I used the rabbinic argument that "man reflects the glory of God and woman reflects the glory of man", was I as a preacher of the gospel interested in fortifying man's arrogance and in putting him up on a pedestal? Was it my vocation to prove the inferiority of women to men?

God forbid! Such a pursuit is unworthy of anyone who claims to be the preacher of the gospel.

It was taught that man should reflect the glory of God in order to place the greater burden on him, who had both public and family obligations, not to engage in activities dishonouring God, God's creation, his wife or his family. And the woman was seen as the glory of man to indicate that she should do nothing that brought dishonour on her husband or her family.

Therefore, if anyone among you uses these discussions from the first decades of the life of the church, in which I was doing no more than giving pastoral guidance to communities in deep uncertainty, to argue the superiority of men over women, let me say as clearly as I can that I will have no part of it.

As for those who are ignorant of how scriptural arguments are used within the Jewish tradition and insist that I have interpreted the story of Adam and Eve for all times, establishing the inferiority of women to men, what can I say but to ask you to bear with their ignorance. But let them leave me out of their evil designs.

Precisely for fear that men, puffed up in their self-importance, might use my admonitions and advice to women as an excuse to lord it over them, I have added at many points what was required of them "in the Lord".

Relationships of love and self-giving

In my letter to the Colossians where I ask wives to be subject to their husbands, I have demanded of the husbands (lest they should think they have control over their wives) that they love their wives and "never treat them harshly" (3:18f.). But more importantly, as a preface to defining these relationships, I laid down the spiritual environment within which all relationships are to be held:

"As God's chosen ones," I demanded of them all, "clothe yourselves with compassion, kindness, humility, meekness and patience. Bear with one another and, if anyone has a complaint against another, forgive each other... Above all, clothe yourself with love which binds everything together in perfect harmony. And let the peace of Christ rule in your hearts, to which indeed you were called" (vv.12-17).

Therefore, to say, "Here is Paul, arguing for the subordination of women to men", is to do violence to me and my intentions. What does kindness have to do with superiority? What does humility have to do with domination?

For the same reason, in my letter to the church in Ephesus I have compared the teaching that the husband is the head of the wife to Christ's being the head of the church (Eph. 5:21-33):

"Husbands love your wives, just as Christ loved the church and gave himself up for her... For this reason a man will leave his father and mother and be joined to his wife, and the two will become one flesh. This is a great mystery, and I am applying it to Christ and his church" (vv.25,31f.).

Do I need to tell you the profound awe and the sense of unspeakable mystery in which I hold the relationship of Christ and the church? Is it not a relationship rooted in a depth of love and self-giving that is beyond all our human understanding?

When we speak about the church as the body of Christ or of Christ as the head of the church, are we not speaking of a communion and unity that passes all human description? Is this a hierarchy, or is it a communion of love? Does "submit" in this relationship mean slavery? Does "love" mean domination?

In comparing the relationship of husband and wife to that of Christ and the church, I insist that the quality of the relationship between a man and woman has been transformed to a new depth of communion "in the Lord". And I have insisted to the Ephesians that everyone should be subject to one another "out of reverence for Christ" (5:21).

Judge for yourself!

The primacy of love

As for me, my conscience is clear. As a Jew I accepted the ordering of the family as it was handed down to me. I interpreted scripture according to the custom of the time. But as one who had come under the power of the gospel, I demanded that all relationships — and I repeat, all relationships — should be subject to the primacy of love.

I dare not preach a gospel that subjects any man or woman to another except in love, for otherwise Christ would have died in vain and the freedom I proclaim would be nothing but falsehood. I repeat, there is no place for subjugation in the gospel, and there is no room for domination in love.

Therefore, my sisters, I say again what I have told you before: Beware of those who tell you, "Paul has ordained that women are subordinate to men; you have to be obedient to what men say"; for they are using scripture to justify their own conclusions. They do not know the gospel. They are out to make mischief and to turn the freedom you have obtained in Christ into slavery. Stand firm against them.

Women's right to speak

4 Through what I am writing here, I am not trying to pretend that I was free of the perceptions and prejudices which men had about women at that time. Indeed, in every letter I wrote, I admitted that a battle was

being fought within me between the "old nature" and the "new", between the "old man" and the "new man", between the powers of darkness and the glorious light of the gospel.

I can say in all honesty, with God as my witness, that I was convinced beyond any doubt that God in Christ loved us all, men and women, equally, and that in the gospel every person and all relationships are transformed and renewed.

It is not without reason that I wrote to the Christians in Galatia that as many of them as were baptized into Christ had clothed themselves with Christ (3:27). And I said that the consequence of this reality is that all the walls which separated us and held us in distorted relationships have been destroyed. It is on this basis that I laid down that "there is no longer Jew or Greek, there is no longer slave or free, there is no longer male and female; for all of you are one in Christ Jesus" (v.28).

Convinced as I was of this truth, was I completely free of the attitude to women that had been ingrained in my "old nature"?

How I wish this had been the case, so that in seeking to resolve the problems in the churches, I would not have fallen back on arguments from the old order of things!

Thus in my first letter to Timothy, in responding to reports that the very same women who were adorning themselves with gold and pearls and fine clothing to impress others were also attempting to take over the leadership and teaching ministry, I came down hard with the general rule that "I permit no woman to teach or to have authority over a man; she is to keep silent" (1 Tim. 2:12).

Although this was provoked by a particular situation in which certain women were acting in ways which were not appropriate for teachers of the gospel, especially in a congregation struggling hard to overcome false teachings, the directive does give the impression that I outlawed women speaking in church. But does this reflect my convictions about women in the church?

But before I take up this question, let me mention a passage in my first letter to the Corinthians (1 Cor. 14:33-36) where there is an even harsher statement: "it is shameful for a woman to speak in church".

I do not know where these words come from; I never wrote them. I was dealing in this chapter with prophecy, and someone has introduced into some of the copies of my letter this prohibition to give it official status.[1]

I remind you again, brothers and sisters, that many of the admonitions and prohibitions in my letters relate to immediate disciplinary problems within the congregations to which I wrote. Often they had to do with false teachings, but also with conflicting claims to leadership and questions of church order.

Especially in congregations drawn from the Gentile community, some women and men were attempting to introduce practices inconsistent with the gospel. To my great dismay, many of them took cover under the "freedom of the gospel" to justify things that were not worthy of the life in the Spirit.

Again, in congregations made up primarily of Christians who came out of Gentile cultures there were many disputes over sexual conduct and practices.

Remember that in all these churches there were also Christians drawn from Jewish stock who were shocked and alienated by some of the conduct being tolerated within these congregations. And in each place the Jewish community — to which I had always gone first with the gospel — was watching closely the life of what I had claimed to be the new community in the Spirit.

In everything that a Christian community did, the witness to the gospel message was at stake.

---

[1] Many New Testament scholars believe that verses 33b to 36 are a later addition and did not belong to Paul's original letter. This interpolation interferes with the smooth flow of the text dealing with prophecy, which moves from verse 33a to 37. This is confirmed by the fact that some ancient manuscripts of the letter do not include verses 33b to 36.

What point am I driving at? I want you to know that in dealing with such a complex situation I sometimes emphasized the freedom of the gospel. But where it was being abused, I advocated admonitions and prohibitions, also to women, which make no sense apart from the context to which they were addressed.

Sometimes I did so to satisfy the Jewish Christians who would otherwise have chosen to leave the fellowship. But in everything I said my goal was to maintain the unity of the church in the bond of peace.

If I admonished women in my letters, I admonished men ten times more! I have even argued that some of them must be put outside the fellowship of the church (1 Cor. 5:1-2).

Therefore, my sisters and brothers, wherever something I have written in those letters helps you in building up the body of the church and guiding it along the path of the gospel, hold on to it. But if anything which was appropriate at that time would diminish the life of the church today, set it aside.

For if we live by the Spirit, let us also walk by the Spirit. For the Spirit you have received is not unable to guide you in your decisions, but is close to you and will lead you where you need to go.

After all, it is not Paul's glory that we are after. Were you baptized in Paul's name? Was Paul crucified for you?

Be guided by the Spirit

I pleaded in my epistles that we live not by the letter but by the Spirit. Do you now wish to accept a new yoke of slavery called "Pauline letters"? Are you so devoid of the Spirit that you cannot discern what the Spirit requires of you today, but must fall back on advice offered two thousand years ago in a culture that is not yours? Has not the Spirit been active among you, taking you to new frontiers of relationships and witness?

Here I am admonishing you again! But it pains me to learn that some of you are saying that Paul has laid down that women should not open their mouths in church and that they are excluded from many aspects of its ministry.

If I prohibited some women in Timothy's church, who cared only for their own glory and self-importance, was I banning all women from ever speaking in church? If I was sometimes unable to overcome my own limitations as a man and, conditioned by my upbringing, spoke about women in ways that diminish them or are not in keeping with the freedom Christ won for them, do you wish to imitate these weaknesses?

Would I be jealous of you if you did better than I have done in announcing the full measure of the gospel? Would it grieve me if all the women and men of the church were to speak of the marvellous deeds that God has done among us in Christ Jesus our Lord?

I ask those who say I have laid down that women should not speak in church to recall the event of Pentecost, when Peter quoted the promise of Joel the prophet that in the last days God would pour his Spirit on all flesh and that their "sons and daughters" would prophesy (Joel 2:28; Acts 2:17). If the Lord poured the Spirit on his daughters so that they might prophesy, who am I to stand in God's way?

This being so, would I have introduced a prohibition on women precisely at the point in my letter to the Corinthians where I discuss the gift of prophecy? Whoever added those verses to some of the copies circulating among the congregations holds a distorted vision of the church.

I did prohibit some women from speaking in the church because of who they were. I have also criticized those whose chattering during the worship disturbed its orderly conduct, and those women who brought dissensions through their gossip. I was harsh on widows and young women who, while remaining outside marriage, behaved in ways that dishonoured their own bodies and the body of the church.

Are women beyond criticism? Do they not have weaknesses that can injure the fellowship of the church?

But if I criticized the women, I criticized the men all the more for their weaknesses and failings. I had the right to criticize both, sometimes with considerable sternness, because they were more than sons and daughters to me in the

22

Lord. They were the fruits of my ministry, God's own gift to my life.

Women's participation in my ministry

In a culture where men were in the leadership in many aspects of society and public life, it is no wonder that most of the preachers and leaders of the church were also men.

But how could I have admonished some women not to speak if there were no women speakers in the church? Would I have had to make an almost general prohibition against women in leadership in Timothy's church if there were no women leaders within the church?

And if I prohibit some women from preaching, does it mean that all women are unsuited to proclaim the message? Have all of them behaved in ways that injured the fellowship?

For I showed equal sternness with men who brought dishonour to the community by giving their bodies to sin through drunkenness and immoral behaviour. Did that disqualify all men from membership in the church? Of course not!

Moreover, I am surprised that some of you say women cannot be in leadership of the church because Paul has prohibited it when you know that I commended to the church in Rome sister Phoebe, who was the deacon of the church at Cenchreae, asking them to "welcome her in the Lord as is fitting for the saints" (Rom. 16:1-3).

I called Prisca (Priscilla) and Aquila, who ministered with me, co-workers "who risked their necks for my life" (vv.3f.). I sent greetings to "Mary who worked very hard" among them (v.6).

Do you suppose that these women who were deacons, leaders and co-workers with me worked in silence, that they never proclaimed the gospel and that they supported me at the risk of their necks without being in leadership?

A whole congregation met regularly at Lydia's home (Acts 16:13-15,40); did this happen without her leading their life?

When I went to Caesarea where I stayed with Philip, one of the evangelists, I found that four of his daughters had the gift of prophecy (Acts 21:9).

And if I said in my letter to the Corinthians that a woman must cover her head when she prays or prophesies in the church, does it not show that women were in fact praying and prophesying in public worship (1 Cor. 11:5)? If the Lord gave women the gift of prophecy, who am I to prevent them?

But let us consider this on a higher plane. We know that there are varieties of gifts, but the same Spirit; and there are varieties of services, but the same Lord. And to each one is given a manifestation of the Spirit for the common good (1 Cor. 12:4-7).

While I have written that these gifts are given to different persons, nowhere have I said that the Spirit endows men with one set of gifts and women with another. For God shows no partiality; in the one Spirit we are all baptized into the one body.

How then can we say in general that women should not open their mouth in the church or exercise leadership within the community?

I urge you, brothers and sisters, to avoid those who cause dissensions and offence, using only some parts of the scripture and taking them out of their historical context to lead you away from the central truth of the gospel. For such people do not serve the Lord.

We do not have a gospel of slavery but of freedom; we are subjected to no one except in the Lord and in the love he commands. And no one can take from us, whether we are men or women, the birthright given to us at our baptism to be the servants of the gospel for the Lord's sake.

To him be the glory forever and unto ages of ages! Amen.

2. Should Women Be in the Ministry?

A Letter to Daniel

Greetings

1 Grace to you and peace from our Lord Jesus Christ, who through his passion and death on the cross has shown the eternal and immeasurable love God has towards us. Let the praise of God ever fill our hearts because, by raising him from the dead, God also manifested to us that we are inheritors of an eternal and imperishable hope, a hope that no human power can remove from our hearts.

Daniel, my beloved friend in the faith, it is to this faith and hope that we have been called, and God through his mercy has entrusted to each one of us the task of ministering to this faith among all God's people.

Controversy over the ministry of women

I am therefore deeply grieved to hear from you that your ministry, which has hitherto been so richly blessed, has come under much pressure because of the controversy raging in your church on the question of the ordination of women into the sacramental ministry of the church.

I am not surprised that this has now become a divisive issue within your congregation. Several churches have already faced this question, and through the theological and spiritual struggle around it they have been enabled to come to terms with the fundamentals of the gospel message itself.

So I encourage you to continue to wrestle with this question, so that the truth of the gospel might become clear in all your deliberations.

I am aware that several of the churches have already called women to the ordained ministry. Others greatly value women's contribution to the life of the church and call them to use their gifts and talents in several forms of service, but have refrained from calling them to the ordained ministry.

It is not my intention to pass judgment on any one of them, although I will not try to conceal where my own thoughts lie.

For this reason I take up the list of objections that you have sent and deal with them one by one for your own edification.

The example set by Jesus

You have written that some among you are insisting that since our Lord called twelve men to be his apostles, it was not his intention that women should be called to the ordained ministry. "If the Lord had wanted women in the ministry," they say, "would he not have called some of those women who closely followed him to be among his twelve apostles?"

But let me ask those who argue this way whether this indeed would have been possible in the times in which our Lord lived. He roamed the hillsides of Galilee proclaiming the kingdom of God. He had "nowhere to lay his head" (Matt. 8:20).

In a society which expected a rabbi to have no dealings with women who were not members of his own family, could our Lord have chosen a group of both women and men to share his life and to go about the cities and villages of Galilee? Does that not expect of him what is impossible in several cultures even today, two thousand years after these events?

Let us be reasonable in what we say. With so many persons and groups waiting to find fault with him, ready to accuse him falsely of flouting the customs and traditions of the people, it would have been impossible for our Lord to have women among the twelve, who lived with him and accompanied him everywhere he went.

What then? Did our Lord limit his ministry to men or have only men as followers? I invite you to read more closely the accounts of his life that have been made available to us since the time I wrote my epistles. Is it not remarkable that so many women in fact followed him, albeit at some distance, quite contrary to the practice of his time?

How else would we account for the women who were healed by him, the women who entered into conversation and even into debate with him? Were not women at the foot of the cross when most of the immediate disciples had fled for fear of arrest?

Do we not read that some women picked up the courage to join Joseph of Arimathea in preparing his body for the hurried burial before sabbath began, and came back at the end of the sabbath to prepare it for its permanent rest (Luke 23:50-24:1)?

Consider the story of Mary and Martha (Luke 10:38-42). Martha chose the role assigned to women by the tradition, busying herself with hospitality matters. She even complained to the Lord that Mary was not playing her traditional role, for Mary had chosen to sit at Jesus' feet to converse with him about the kingdom.

And how did our Lord reply? "Mary has chosen the better part," he said, "which will not be taken away from her!"

I urge those who argue that the Lord never intended women to be in the ministry to think deeply about this story. Mary and Martha represent two distinct roles, and is it not significant that, while not despising Martha's love, the Lord affirmed Mary's interest in the kingdom as choosing the "better part", which would not be taken away from her?

But women appear to have done more than listening to him. Luke has recorded that while Jesus "went on through cities and villages, proclaiming and bringing the good news of the kingdom of God, the twelve were with him, *as well as some women* who had been cured of evil spirits and infirmities" (Luke 8:1-3).

And what is more, he recalls that it was women like Mary Magdalene, and Joanna, the wife of Herod's steward Chuza, and Susanna and many others "who provided for him out of their resources" (v.3).

Or consider this. Of all the acts of love and discipleship done to our Lord, he commended the action of the woman who anointed him as the one that will be remembered "wherever this good news is proclaimed in the whole world" (Matt. 26:13).

The first witness of the resurrection

It is recorded that on the third day our Lord appeared beside the empty tomb to Mary Magdalene, and asked her "to go to the disciples and to tell them" that he had risen. What joy it must have been for Mary Magdalene to be the first to see the risen Lord and to proclaim, "I have seen the Lord", to his disciples (John 20:18)!

Let no one dismiss this as unimportant to the issue we are looking at. You recall Simon's confession that Jesus was indeed the Messiah. The Lord's response to him, "You are Peter, and on this rock I will build my church" (Matt. 16:18), is one of the arguments that has been used to build the case for the primacy of the Petrine ministry. How much more importance should we attach to the first instruction Jesus gave as the risen Lord!

If Jesus assigned to a woman the task of telling the disciples of his resurrection, who are we to prevent women from this primary calling? Could this text not be used to argue that after the resurrection it was on the witness of women that Jesus intended to build his church?

And if I claim, on the basis of having encountered the Lord on the road to Damascus, the right to apostleship, does Mary Magdalene not have an even greater claim as the one who first saw the risen Lord and was entrusted with the task of announcing his resurrection to the disciples?

Am I being frivolous? Am I trying to argue for argument's sake? By no means! I am only trying to show you that so often we use the scripture to confirm what we already want to believe.

If the risen Lord had appeared first to Peter and said, "Go and tell the disciples that I am risen", that would have been used as another major argument that Peter was the first among the disciples, because it was to him that Jesus first appeared; it was he who was asked to "go and tell". Would not a case have been built that it was the Lord's very intention that he should be the first witness?

If this had indeed been the case, one can even imagine hearing the argument that Jesus never intended women to be witnesses, because if he had intended them to be, he would have appeared to them as the risen Lord.

So what shall we say, now that scripture *does* bear witness that he made a woman the first witness and commissioned her to go and tell the news to the disciples?

Why do those who argue that Jesus would have chosen a woman to be among the twelve, if he had intended them to be ministers, keep silent about this story of the first witness?

Or are we using scripture to confirm our own practices and prejudices?

But I have no interest in winning arguments by quoting scripture. The scriptures are written so that we might be edified, not so that we might prove our points. What I have sought to show you thus far is that those who say, "But the Lord chose only twelve men as disciples", are not reading their scriptures carefully enough. Given the times in which these things happened and the fact that all the gospel narratives were written by men, it is significant that women appear so prominently in Jesus' ministry.

The church, a community of women and men

What is at stake here is much more than whether or not Jesus had women disciples. Those who have challenged you on the question of women in the ministry raise searching questions about the meaning of the church and its ministry.

Are women and men equally part of the one body of Christ? As I have said in my earlier letters, the Spirit does give different gifts — some to be apostles, some teachers, some prophets, some healers and some miracle workers and so on.

Not everyone is called to all the ministries of the church; not everyone is endowed with the gifts and charismata needed for the different services required within the body of Christ. Can everyone be a priest? Then where is the congregation? If everyone were a prophet, to whom would prophecy be made?

No, as it is, we know that the Spirit calls different persons to different ministries so that all the ministries together might fulfill the common calling and be exercised for the common good of the one body.

But nowhere have I said that these gifts are given according to one's gender. If all the spiritual gifts and ministries I spoke about in my earlier letters were meant only for men, are women without the Spirit? Are they not also endowed with gifts?

But since I did not list some gifts as special gifts of women, does it not follow that I did not see that God makes any distinction between men and women in the call to the ministry? Or do we expect women to play no role at all in the life of the church? The prophet Joel proclaimed the promise that God would "pour down his Spirit on all flesh" so that our "sons and daughters would prophesy". Does God go back on promises? Is it from jealousy that we object when God calls women to do those ministries we feel are reserved for men alone?

Would that all God's people were prophets!

Remember Moses and the tent of meeting. The Lord had commanded him to gather seventy elders into the tent of meeting so that the Spirit that filled Moses might also rest upon them. But when the Spirit fell, it also came upon Eldad and Medad, who had chosen to remain in the camp, and they too began to prophesy.

When Joshua, son of Nun, asked Moses to forbid them, how did Moses respond? "Are you jealous for my sake?", he asked Joshua. "Would that all of Lord's people were prophets, and that the Lord would put his Spirit on them!" (Num. 11:24-30).

So, my son, I have no reason to believe that God refrains from calling women to any aspect of the ministry of the church. Who are we to set limits to God's calling? If it pleased God that the Spirit should rest on those in the camp as on those in the tent of meeting, let us rejoice with Moses and say, "Would that all God's people were prophets!"

The priest: the icon of Jesus the man

2 You have mentioned that some among you do not dispute that the grace of God is bestowed equally on women and men, but believe that priesthood is a gift and calling limited to men.

I perceive that those who hold this view have nothing against women, but believe that the priest, as a true representative of Christ the man, must be a man.

The priest, they hold, is the icon of Jesus the Christ. In so far as Jesus was male, they understand maleness as an essential part of exercising a priestly ministry.

"When so many other ministries of the church are open to women", they ask, "why are some women eager to take up the one ministry more appropriate for men, that of truly representing Christ at the altar? This is not a matter of privilege, but of faithful representation."

How then do we understand the gospel? When the evangelist wrote that "the Word became flesh and lived among us" (John 1:14), was he not speaking about God's taking *human* form so that all human life might be transformed in Christ Jesus?

Jesus was of course a man; he could not have been both a man and a woman at the same time. But does not the humanity that Christ assumed include both the male and female ways of being a human being?

Are women without any hope?

Consider this. Your own philosophers have taught that in Jesus Christ God assumed humanity in order to redeem it. "That which he assumed, that he redeemed," it has been said.

If the humanity that Jesus assumed is so tied up with his being a male, are we saying that he redeemed only half of humankind? Should we wait for God to take female flesh so that the women among us might also be redeemed? Are we not making a mockery of the incarnation when we give more importance to the maleness of Jesus than to the humanity which he embraced?

In my own letters I have talked of Jesus as the new Adam, the one who transformed the old humanity into a new one. I have written that "just as one man's trespass led to condemnation for all, so one man's act of righteousness leads to justification and life for all. For just as by the one man's disobedience the many were made sinners, so by the one man's obedience the many will be made righteous" (Rom. 5:18f.).

What did I mean by the "one man"? Was I not following the Genesis story, which says, "God created man *(Adam), male and female* he created them"?

If sin had been brought into the world by the male, it would have been justified that God assumed maleness in order to redeem it, and women would have been without sin. But since sin came through "the one man", including the male and female, then the "new man" also must embrace the male and the female.

Set your eyes on higher things

Am I suggesting that there are no differences between men and women? Am I insisting that there are no special gifts that we bring to the life of the church as women and as men? Am I advocating that women can truly serve the church only by becoming priests?

By no means. All I want to insist is that "all of us", whether male or female, "who have been baptized into Christ Jesus were baptized into his death. Therefore we have been buried with him by baptism into his death, so that, just as Christ was raised from the dead by the glory of the Father, so we too might walk in newness of life" (Rom. 6:2-4).

What then are we to say? Now that Christ is risen from the dead, "we regard no one from a human point of view"; and "even though we once knew Christ from the human point of view, we know him no longer in that way" (2 Cor. 5:16).

How then can we place so much emphasis on the maleness of Jesus? Do we not know that flesh and blood do not inherit the kingdom of God?

Let us set our eyes on higher things. We know that God is not a respecter of persons, and that everyone who turns in repentance and faith, whether male or female, has the promise of everlasting life.

And that promise is sealed by the Spirit. "For all who are led by the Spirit of God are children of God." We do not have a spirit of slavery to fall back into fear, but the spirit of adoption; and the Spirit bears witness with our spirit that we are the children of God (Rom. 8:12-17).

Thus God has reconciled each one of us, men and women, and has given to us all the ministry of reconciliation so that "we are ambassadors for Christ, since God is making his appeal through us" (2 Cor. 5:18-21).

Are we saying that all these things are said only about the males among us?

On the traditions of the church

3 You have written that of all the arguments against calling women to the ordained ministry, the one you find strongest is that which is drawn from tradition: that we must maintain the unbroken tradition of the church of ordaining only men into the ministry.

Tradition is indeed important. We are not called to make up our faith; and what I passed on to you is what I had received from the Lord. As I wrote to the Corinthians, only one foundation has been laid, Jesus Christ. All who seek to build must build on this one foundation, and those who build on any other foundation do not know the gospel.

Therefore, the church of Christ is not built on any human wisdom or imagination, but is rooted in the faith of the apostles and prophets, saints and martyrs who have gone before us.

What then? I have warned before, and I warn you again, about those who come to you with high-sounding words of wisdom, ever ready to lead you astray, and about those who would tempt you to be conformed to what the world would have us do. We are not to be tossed about to and fro by every wind of doctrine; nor are we called to keep pace with all the changes and desires of the world.

You know that from the very beginning of the church there have been many wolves in sheep's clothing, ever ready to lead people away from what has been received by announcing a new message that is different from the glorious gospel revealed in Christ Jesus.

I have pleaded with the churches to resist these people, so that they not be led back into the slavery from which they were redeemed.

I appeal to you, therefore, not to quarrel among yourselves over the importance of tradition, but to examine it together in the light of the gospel.

I am not unaware that some of the sisters and brothers among you are examining the tradition more closely to ascertain whether the role played by women in the leadership of the church in times past was not in fact greater than is often believed.

Be that as it may, I want you to know what happened to me in my understanding of tradition as I struggled to spread the gospel among all people.

Called out of a tradition

You are aware how zealous I was for my own traditions. When I saw that the gospel preached by the apostles challenged the traditions in which I was brought up, I became a persecutor of the church, and was ready to go as far as Damascus to bind those who followed the new way.

But God, who even before I was born set me apart to be an apostle, revealed Christ Jesus to me on the road to Damascus, and commissioned me, unworthy as I was, to preach the gospel to the ends of the earth.

You are also aware how proud I was of the heritage into which I was born, how I was steeped in the study of the law, how much I valued the faith of our forebears and the traditions handed down to us over generations.

But when I was faced with the challenge of the grace of God offered in Christ Jesus our Lord, I had little choice but to see the gospel as having primacy over the tradition that had shaped me.

Thus I who had been the persecutor of the church for the sake of tradition became a fugitive from those who would persecute me in defence of that tradition.

In spite of this, I did not abandon my Jewish tradition, but struggled hard, as you have seen in my letter to the Romans (chs 9-11), to own my tradition in the light of the gospel, so that the olive branch of the gospel grafted into the stem might bear the fruits of faith.

Controversy over tradition

Besides this, you know that within the early church there were those who wanted to preserve tradition by insisting that all Gentiles who accepted Christ would have to be circumcised as the mark of belonging to the covenant community. In their zeal to preserve the traditions of the ancestors they were ready to impose circumcision also on the Gentile believers.

But could zeal for the tradition be allowed to challenge the foundation of the gospel: that God, through the love shown for us in Christ Jesus, justifies us by our faith? And could the desire to preserve tradition be permitted to endanger the oneness of the community created by the gospel message? By no means!

I spared no effort in confronting the traditionalists in order to maintain the truth of the gospel (Acts 15). If God has bestowed the same grace on both Jews and Gentiles who have accepted the gospel, then tradition must give way to the truth that in Christ Jesus, God has broken down the barriers between the Jews and the Greeks.

The freedom of the Spirit

I appeal to you therefore to consider the nature of the grace that has been given to you.

Has God not bestowed liberating grace on both men and women? Are not all, irrespective of their gender, incorporated into the one body of Christ, the church? Does the Spirit not grant gifts to all God's people without distinction based on gender? Does the fruit of the Spirit not become manifest in any person who abides in Christ?

If this is so, how then can we prevent women who feel compelled by the Spirit from exercising the ministry to which they are called? Who has made us arbiters between God and God's people?

Am I then saying that anyone who claims to be called by God should immediately be accepted into the ministry of the church? Am I advocating that the community of faith make no test to see if the calling is indeed from the Lord? Am I saying that every woman is capable of bearing the image of Christ before the altar?

By no means! Not everyone who claims to be called by God is suitable to represent our common humanity before God.

But I submit that to say women cannot be ordained to the ministry *because they are women* is to put at risk the truth of the gospel. For at no point in the proclamation of the gospel as God's message of salvation, or in the experience of redemption in the life of the people, has gender been an issue. The gospel message and the call to bear witness to it are not addressed to men only, but to the whole people of God.

I repeat again: even though it is evident that the Spirit bestows different gifts on different people, we are told nowhere in the scripture that the Spirit is poured out on us differently according to the gender to which we belong.

And if, as Peter says in his letter, God has made us all into "a royal priesthood, a holy nation, God's own people" in order that we may "proclaim the mighty acts of him who called us out of darkness into his marvellous light" (1 Pet. 2:9), then a tradition which limits the possibility of women to exercise this calling stands under the judgment of this very message.

For it is to every Christian that Peter says, "Once you were not a people, but now you are God's people; once you had not received mercy, but now you have received mercy" (v. 10).

Ritual cleanliness

4 Some members of your church have raised with you the question of ritual purity, pointing to the fact that the book of Leviticus (ch. 15) teaches that a woman

who has a regular discharge of blood from her body remains ritually impure for seven days. Similarly, ritual impurity is also prescribed in relation to childbirth.

"If everything a woman touches during this period also becomes unclean," they ask, "how is it possible for a woman to open the scripture or to touch the sacraments during this period?"

First, let me point out that the laws concerning ritual impurity in the book of Leviticus concern not only women but also men. Any man who has a bodily discharge or emission of semen is considered unclean for a period, and ritual washing is expected of him before he becomes clean again (Lev. 15:13-18).

But let us not quarrel over this. What do you think? If God has created the human body so that we might "be fruitful and multiply" through natural processes as ordained at creation, would the very processes that make this possible be considered unclean in God's eyes (Gen. 1:28)?

Insofar as these words from Leviticus deal with all bodily discharges of both men and women, are we not dealing here with rules of hygiene in the life of an ancient civilization?

And why do we single out this one regulation from among the thousands prescribed in the books of Moses, when on other matters we say that it is the grace of God and the response of faith which mark us out as the church? What steps have those who are so zealous for ritual purity put in place to ensure that the men at the altar are ritually clean?

How is it that those who claim to be free from the law because their sins have been cleansed by the blood of Christ associate blood with impurity when it comes to women, and go back to the law from which they claim to have been freed?

One of the hymns you sing when you celebrate the birth of our Lord says of Christ: "Lo! he abhors not the virgin's womb." If God chose pregnancy and childbirth as the way to enter human history, let us no longer consider them unclean.

The purity that the Lord requires

For the prophets and our Lord himself have taught us that purity is of the heart, and it is not things from outside but our thoughts and desires that make us pure or impure before the Lord.

Let us therefore no longer act like immature persons, putting stumbling blocks and hindrances in each other's way. Instead, let us try to discern what is well-pleasing in God's sight.

In all humility let us support one another. And let us not be too quick to judge, for judgment belongs to the Lord. For by grace you have been saved through faith, and this is not your own doing; it is the gift of God.

Concluding advice

Daniel, my beloved child in the faith, I give thanks for every remembrance of you, because I know that you have so far led the people committed to your charge wisely and in the fear of God.

Do not allow this controversy over the ordination of women to the sacramental ministry to destroy the life of the church. But with patience help the contending parties to understand one another so that they might grow into a fuller measure of faith and into a community of women and men in the church, witnessing to the power of the gospel to break down every wall that has been built among us.

And now may the God of peace, who by the raising of Christ Jesus from the dead has given us an everlasting hope, strengthen your spirit and guide you in all your thoughts and actions.

And may glory, honour, praise and thanksgiving be unto our God for ever and ever. Amen.

3. Are We Not Ashamed?

A Second Letter to the Christians

Greetings

1 Paul, called to be an apostle of Jesus Christ by the will of God, to all the churches to which teams of messengers have been sent over the past few years: Grace to you and peace from God who has loved you with an everlasting love and from the Lord Jesus Christ whom you serve.

I give thanks to God for all the good things I have heard about you, especially for those of you who live as minority communities in the midst of many who do not profess the name of Christ, yet hold fast to your faith against many odds.

I have been told by the brothers and sisters who came to visit you that many of you have not lost your zeal to proclaim the gospel and that you serve the communities in which you live with dedication and love.

May the Lord's name be praised and may you be strengthened by the Spirit to persevere to the end, so that you may be found blameless on the day of our Lord Jesus Christ.

God who has called you is faithful; in everything you do, put your trust in God's faithfulness so that you might never lose courage in facing the trials of this earthly life.

Violence against women

Now concerning some of the matters brought to my attention, I have been told by the groups that visited the churches that violence against women is widespread in many societies.

I am even more dismayed to hear that physical violence against women is also prevalent among Christians in many churches. Some of the testimony from women and groups of women about how they are treated by men can bring nothing but disgrace to the life of the whole church.

I am astonished to hear that some of the men among you justify such physical violence by saying that women are required by the scripture to be subordinate to men, so that if a wife does not obey her husband, he has the right to beat her into obedience!

I was ashamed to hear that one of you has even said that such beating of one's wife, by aiding her to fulfill what is required of her, helps her in her own salvation!

How can this state of affairs be tolerated within the body of Christ? Words fail me, because it is against everything I had hoped would happen in the relationship between women and men through the proclamation of the gospel.

Anyone who says that in the advice I gave to the churches that wives should obey or submit to their husbands I was giving authority to men over the bodies of women is distorting the entire intention of my whole ministry.

As I have written to you in my earlier letter, while I accepted a hierarchy of relationships, I understood this relationship to be fully transformed by the gospel (1 Cor. 11:11f.).

Have I not pleaded that we must submit ourselves to one another in the Lord (Eph. 5:21)? Have I not insisted that the husband has no more authority over his wife's body than the wife has over her husband's body, and that sexual relationships are to be based on mutual consent (1 Cor. 7:3-5)? How I have pleaded with the churches that husbands love their wife and honour them!

How then can you say that the scriptures justify physical violence against women?

When I compared the relationship of husband and wife to that of Christ and the church, I elevated that relationship to a mystery of profound self-giving love, which requires of the husband the same kind of self-offering that Christ showed on the cross for the church.

How I wish I was with you in person, so that I could reprimand you directly and admonish those who are distorting the intention of my letters in this way! For those of you who advocate this are destroying the glorious relationships opened to us as women and men through the message of the gospel.

What right have you?

In any case, what right have you to touch another person who is also created in the image of God? Who gives you the authority to use physical violence against someone for whom Christ has died and has made his own?

I have said that our bodies are temples of the Holy Spirit and for that reason they should not be defiled (1 Cor. 6:19). If this is so, how can you use violence against that in which the Spirit of God resides?

If I am angry with you, my anger is justified. I do not want to be associated in any way with any man who disrespects another person who is equally a child of God and uses her as if he owns her as one would own a piece of property.

And I am even more angry if these worthless men say that it is my own teaching that justifies their ungodly behaviour!

Let me make myself clear. I permit no man to touch a woman in his anger, or use force against her in their sexual relationships. And if any man persists in using violence against women, the women should bring this matter to the public, and should ask the community to deal with the matter. Such men should be put to shame.

If any pastor or teacher among you practises or advocates violence against women, he should be removed from being a minister of the church. He has lost the right to serve the cause of the gospel; he has no knowledge of the love of Christ made manifest on the cross.

For what has the cross to do with power? What has love to do with violence? What does self-giving have in common with domination?

No. I urge you to remove the cancer from the body so that the whole body might not be affected.

Advice to women

To the women among you, I repeat my advice that you respect your husbands even as they are expected to respect you. Do not provoke them to anger by harsh words or insults, because violence and hurt caused by insults, rudeness and wilful neglect go deep and are even more difficult to heal.

Men who are verbally insulted turn their anger into physical violence, and make a habit of it. Do everything that is possible to build your relationship on love and mutual respect and to maintain peace and harmony with those among whom you live.

If you are married, take your rightful role in the bringing up of your children. Do not neglect them; they are God's gift to you.

From the very beginning, expect of your husband to be co-responsible in bringing up the children.

Treat all your children, male or female, equally; and teach your sons to respect their sisters, so that when they grow up they will have learned to respect their wives.

But if your husband perpetrates physical violence against you in anger or in drunkenness, do not take it as God's will for you or believe that the scripture has commanded you to obey and submit to him irrespective of what he does.

This is not the scripture, and he has no such authority over your body. And as the child of God, you have the right not to be violated.

If you do not succeed in your own attempts to put the situation right, first share it with your sisters in the congregation, so that you may be strengthened in your suffering; then bring it to the open so that the community of faith might deal with it.

For by suffering in silence you are not helping your husband to be redeemed. It is secrecy that helps such men to continue in their evil ways and thus become unworthy of the gospel in the sight of God.

An appeal

Therefore, by the grace given to me in Jesus Christ, I again appeal to you, husbands and wives, to build your relationship on mutual respect and love.

Let your love be genuine, so that when differences arise among you they might be resolved through conversation and mutual understanding. Do not provoke one another to anger.

Be ready when necessary to suffer wrong, if by so doing your relationships are restored. In humility bear one another's burdens, so that the love of Christ may fill your hearts.

Witness of the church

2 Now concerning the wider community, it has been reported that there are many other evils perpetrated against girls and women which have implications for your life in the community and for your Christian witness among the people.

Some of the groups that visited the churches have reported about the evils of discrimination against the female child, to the point of their being abandoned and allowed to die at birth. In other situations, preference is given to male children in providing the basic needs of food, clothing and education.

In some of your countries girls are sold into marriage as children, and those who grow up to be women are subjected to a dowry system that treats women as a commodity.

I want to remind you of the people who first brought the message of the gospel into some of your lands. While some of them were oblivious to these social evils and even contributed to them indirectly, most of them struggled hard to alleviate the sufferings of women and girl children.

Preaching of the gospel did much to enhance the place of women. It brought education to girls; it prevented women from the requirement of throwing themselves on the funeral pyre of their husbands; it alleviated the sufferings of widows.

If this was the heritage of those who first preached the gospel in your lands, what is your own witness today in your society?

You who pride yourselves on making converts of other people, what have you gained for the kingdom if these evils are allowed to persist among the people to whom you minister? Is the preaching of the gospel about making converts, or is it about bringing wholeness into the life of peoples and communities?

It grieves me to hear from those who visited you that many churches are far behind even those who do not fear

God in confronting these evils and in advocating the rights of women in such societies.

Where is your Christian witness? Where is your message that each person is precious in the sight of God? Where is your concern for each and every person for whose liberation and life Christ gave himself on the cross?

I am not writing like this to make you ashamed, my brothers and sisters, but to admonish you for having become self-sufficient and complacent in the life you lead in the community.

Do not lose the rich heritage that is yours as those who brought the message of God's liberation into situations of bondage.

Do not be conformed to the world, but be transformed by the renewing of your minds, so that you may know the will and purpose of God for those among whom you live.

Persevere in your ministry of healing; stand firm against evil; seek justice and correct oppression.

Remember what prophet Micah has written: "He has told you, O mortal, what is good; and what does the Lord require of you but to do justice, and to love kindness and to walk humbly with your God?" (6:8).

Child prostitution

3 It has actually been reported to me that in some countries girls and boys as young as eight years of age are often sold into child prostitution because of poverty, and that many men from countries where the church has taken root go to abuse these children for their pleasure.

To churches in countries from where men travel to exploit the poverty of the people and violate the innocence of children elsewhere, I say, even if these men are not part of the Christian community, you are responsible to do everything you can so that this hideous and repulsive practice is rooted out.

I have already written that a man who is united to a prostitute dishonours his body and is not worthy of the kingdom (1 Cor. 6:12-20). What then can we say of those who in their insatiable sexual appetite violate children and destroy their lives even before they begin to blossom?

I appeal to you, my brothers and sisters, with all the authority I can muster as the messenger of the gospel, that you do everything that you can to remove this practice.

I am aware that some among you have already undertaken a ministry of meeting this challenge, and I commend you on the basis of the excellent reports I have of you. You are doing this because you love the Lord and seek to do what is right. Your names are written in the book of Life.

To those of you in countries from where these children are taken into this form of slavery, I ask that you do everything you can to change the conditions of life and the attitude that parents have to their children, so that they are not led astray into selling their children for a price.

Do not hesitate to challenge the authority of the state in this matter, because the state is there to protect the people, especially the vulnerable.

To all of you, I appeal that you see these children as your own and do all you can to end their suffering. Let this be a part of your Christian ministry in the community.

The appeal to culture

4 You know that it was for your benefit that groups were sent among you by the churches around the world. They came to enable you to examine your own life as churches concerning the place of women in church and society.

I am astonished to hear that many of you have mentioned the culture in which you live as the reason for the plight of women in both church and society.

You know that in my ministry and in my letters I defended the right of Christians from a Jewish background to remain in their own tradition. At the same time, I resisted firmly those who insisted that Gentile Christians must accept Jewish customs and practices in order to be part of the church.

In so doing, I have tried to show that the kingdom of God is not about outward things but about the transformation of our lives through our participation in the life and death of Christ, who gave himself for us on the cross.

I have insisted in my letter to the Romans that we are not justified by anything that our own cultures and traditions have to offer us. God justifies us by our faith in Christ, and the Spirit is poured into our hearts so that we may gradually be transformed into the full measure of the stature of Christ (Rom. 6-8).

Avoid false hopes

I wrote these things so that the Christians in Rome, whether Jews or Gentiles, might know that becoming a Christian did not oblige them to disown their culture or their people.

At the same time, I tried to show that insofar as we are incorporated into the body of Christ and made by God to be heirs of a glory that is yet to be revealed, we no longer see the world only from the human point of view.

For we know how sin clings to all our ways of life and the human institutions and cultures that we have created. For when we want to do good, evil is at hand; and what we do is not the good which we want to do but the evil which we do not want to do.

Why is this so? Why do humans so easily resort to violence? Why do our nations so readily engage in self-destructive violence and war to resolve differences?

The reason is obvious. Even though the grace of God is here, sin still besets us. As I have written, creation itself is subjected to futility and groans as if in labour pains to be redeemed from its bondage to decay, in order to obtain the freedom of the glory of the children of God (Rom. 8:18-25).

Therefore, even though we live in the world as we do, we do not pin our hopes on what the world has to offer in its cultures and traditions. Rather, we are co-workers with God for its transformation, so that we and the world may both be changed into the likeness of what God has intended from the beginning.

Do not be conformed to the world

What then am I saying? Culture in itself is not to be rejected, for there may be much good in culture. But human cultures also participate in sin and are in need of redemption.

While the God who loves the world has called us to live in the world, we are also called not to be conformed to the world, but to be transformed, by the renewing of our minds.

How then can we say that we have no choice but to be conformed to cultures that make women into pieces of property or deny them their God-given self-respect and dignity?

Are we not casting doubt on the power of the gospel if we do no more than throw up our hands in despair and say, "This is part of our people's culture, and there is very little to be done about it"?

Where then is our ministry of transformation? Where is our message that brings hope to those in bondage? Where is our power, as co-workers with God, to heal, to restore and to re-create?

Brothers and sisters, I am not unmindful of the dimensions of the task I am talking about, for this is not just a matter of human frailty, but of confronting powers and forces of darkness that militate against what God intends for the world we live in.

I am aware that some of you who struggle for the cause of women have been accused of flouting the traditions of your people. You have been reprimanded as those who introduce attitudes, practices and policies with regard to the status and role of women that would destroy the culture handed down by the forebears.

There are instances of women who advocate the humanity of other women being accused of losing their femininity and of men who support them being held in suspicion and disdain by other men. Many men fear that the hold of power they have over women would be lost by changing the way things are.

Can we betray the gospel?

What then can we say? Are we to deny the gospel for the sake of a culture that stands in contradiction to its primary message? Are we to compromise with evil for fear of alienating the community we live in?

You must answer for yourselves. I do not pretend to have answers to these questions on your behalf, because I know that all our cultures are different, and cherished values of some cultures have been destroyed in the name of the gospel by those who lacked the wisdom to discern them.

There can indeed be advocacy for women which is irresponsible, which refuses to see the deeper wisdom ingrained in a culture. There are times when we must defend the values preserved by our cultures against what is being imposed by those who claim to know better — even as I did in defence of the Gentile Christians.

But let this not be an excuse. We know what the gospel is about; we know that Christ has abolished the barriers between us; and we know that God has called us into a community of men and women in which everyone's dignity as the child of God is to be preserved and protected.

Discrimination within the church

For this reason, I was distressed to hear that forms of discrimination practised against women in the wider society are also allowed, in the name of culture, within some of your churches.

Thus, it has been reported to me that some of you do not allow women even to serve on church committees, claiming that it is not the practice of the people among whom you live to give leadership positions to women or to see them as having equal rights with men.

Are your hearts so hardened that you are unable to hear the will and purpose of God for all God's children? The gospel message and the Spirit of God are there to guide you in your relationships: why do you look for guidance to a culture that is yet to be redeemed? Or are you taking cover behind culture for your inability to measure up to the demands the gospel makes on you?

Beloved in the Lord, I do not challenge you in this way to hurt your feelings or to put you on the defensive. For I gain nothing for the gospel if I bring only accusations against you and earn the name of someone who pontificates from a distance, not knowing the realities in which you live.

Christian witness in danger

Consider this. What witness are we giving to the truth of the gospel message if our lives and relationships are no better than those among whom we live? Why would men or women want to embrace the gospel, unless in so doing their relationships are transformed into something that enhances their dignity and worth? If the Christian community practises all the kinds of discrimination seen within the human community, where is our witness?

What then are we saying about ourselves? Are we without a liberating message? Is the body of Christ no different from the culture in which it lives? Do we continue in our old relationships beset by sin as if Christ had not died on the cross to transform them?

God forbid! Let us put away our old selves and, as children who have received a higher calling, put on the nature of Christ. Let us love one another as God has loved us. And let our relationships be truly mutual, knowing that we are all equally sons and daughters in the sight of God.

Let us put everyone's talents to full use so that the cause of the kingdom may be served well in all our cultures.

Our stand should be clear to all. We are not against culture, but we do not support oppression. We cherish the heritage handed down to us, but we serve the Lord. We respect all people, but are subject to none. We are in this world, but we are not of it. In all things we do, we seek to honour no one other than God, who alone is the judge of all nations.

To the same God, who by raising Christ Jesus from the dead has called us to new relationships, be honour, glory, praise and thanksgiving for ever and ever. Amen.

4. Are the Scriptures Inspired?

A Letter to Marcus

Greetings

Paul to Marcus, a faithful servant of the word: Grace to you and peace from our Lord Jesus Christ.

I give thanks to God for every remembrance of you, because I have heard of the diligence with which you serve the people committed to your charge.

I know how you have been taught the scriptures from your childhood, and how you have come to love the word of God, seeking its guidance in everything you do. Your knowledge of and passion for the Bible are known among all who live with me.

The authority to interpret the scriptures

I am therefore distressed to learn from the letter you have sent me that you are disheartened by the way the scripture is being interpreted, especially in relation to the question of women in the life and ministry of the church.

Those who live with me have urged me to respond at once, for they want you to know that we are not among those who undermine the authority of scripture or consider it outdated for the times in which we live.

Nor are we seeking to make the scripture say what we would like to believe. For that would be the work of ungodly people who want scriptural authority to justify the desires of their own hearts.

On the contrary, as you well know, we are among those who have put their trust in the Lord. We have made the eternal love God has shown in Christ Jesus our own. At much risk to our own lives we defend the truth of the gospel among people who deny it.

Not that the gospel needs our defence, nor does it stand or fall by what we say or do. But as ones enslaved by the love of Christ we stand under its judgment. Woe to us if we deny the gospel!

In fact, our interest has been to show how the gospel, to which the scriptures bear testimony, is as relevant today as it was to those who had the joy of hearing it in the early days.

I beg you therefore not to be misled by those who accuse us falsely of distorting the scriptures, but to listen to what we have to say with an open heart.

We do not insist that your heart find conformity with ours — except of course in love — for who are we to pretend to know the true meaning of scriptures? And what right do we have to expect that everyone should agree with us?

From the very beginning, the church has believed that the Holy Spirit, the one promised by Christ, would take what he had taught and interpret it to us, as the one who leads us into all truth.

Although individuals have always interpreted the scripture, it is the community gathered in the name of Christ which has finally received an interpretation as given by the Spirit.

We are nothing more than servants of the word of God.

Are not all scriptures inspired?

You have reminded me that I myself wrote in an earlier letter that all scripture is inspired by God and given for our instruction (2 Tim. 3:16).

How then, you ask, can I now say that some of what I wrote, which the church has accepted as scripture, reflected my own thoughts, limited by my own culture? If the scripture as we have it requires women to cover their heads in church, can we now say that this was meant for women of that time and does not bind women today?

"Do the authority and meaning of the eternal word of God change because we would like to make accommodations for women?", you ask. "Can we set aside the word of God because it seems to contradict what we think should be done?"

What can I say to this? Do I believe that the word of God should be changed to meet the desires of our hearts? Am I arguing that it is no longer relevant to us because we live in different times? Am I asking people to set aside the scriptures so that we can teach whatever we want about women in the church today?

God forbid! If anything, what concerns me most in these days is that the scripture is not widely read by Christians, and there is so little knowledge of what it teaches.

How I long for all the children of God to know the scriptures and live by them, to have them written in their hearts and minds so that they might do what is pleasing in God's sight!

What then am I saying? Am I contradicting myself, saying different things at different times? Am I adding to your confusion rather than dealing with the issues you have raised?

Fulfilling the intention of scripture

Take the example of our Lord himself. "Do not think I have come to abolish the law or the prophets," he said. "I have come not to abolish but to fulfill" (Matt. 5:17).

It is the same Lord who also said, "You have heard that it was said, 'an eye for an eye and a tooth for a tooth'. But I say to you, do not resist an evildoer. But if anyone strikes you on the right cheek, turn the other also" (Matt. 5:38).

If the law of God as given in the scriptures says that "an eye for an eye, and a tooth for a tooth" is what is just in responding to the evil done to us, how could Jesus say to his followers, "But I say to you..."?

Was he not going beyond what is laid down in scripture? Was he not breaking the law and — as indeed he was accused of doing — "abolishing the scriptures and teaching things against what our ancestors have taught us"?

What do you think? If Jesus claimed that he had come not to destroy but to fulfill the law, was he right in changing what Moses had laid down in scripture? Was he not casting doubt on the possibility that scripture could guide and inspire people who lived in his time, many centuries after Moses gave the scriptures?

We know this is not the case, because God approved Jesus at his baptism with the proclamation, "This is my beloved son, with whom I am well pleased" (Matt. 3:17). Jesus himself had no other intention than to fulfill the will of God.

Our Lord was fulfilling the scripture by fulfilling its intention. For he knew that at the time when Moses gave this law, some men were ready to take their opponents' very lives in revenge for an eye that was lost.

If Moses, to deal with the hardness of the heart of some, laid down scriptural guidance that limits the extent of revenge, would he not have been pleased if the one who lost his eye would turn to his brother and say, "I forgive you, because you did it in a fit of anger"?

In this instance, would not the breaking of the letter of the law itself becomes the fulfilment of its intention? Would God not rejoice over one who went beyond the law to be faithful to what it intends?

So it is with all scripture, including those letters of mine which have become part of it.

If at one moment in history I asked women to submit themselves to their husbands and to obey them, would I be displeased if husbands and wives submitted themselves to each other in love and truly honoured one another by listening to each other? Was this not what I was hoping for in calling for mutual submission "in the Lord"?

Or will God be displeased and hold that you are going against scripture if you show greater love and respect for one another?

Let us be reasonable. What is it that we want to defend? Is it the law, or what it intends? Is it the letter, or the spirit behind it? Our Lord was most critical of those who despise people in order to be right with the written word.

For this reason, the literal application of scripture as the word of God is looked down upon in my own Jewish tradition, and we have rabbis to interpret and apply the scripture for different situations.

If the word of God were only to be applied as written down, with no thought for what it might mean today, why has God given us intelligence? Why should it be studied? Why have there been teachers, preachers and prophets who interpret what is written? Why would Jesus say to his followers, "But I say to you…"? Why was the

Spirit given to us as an "interpreter" to lead us "into all truth"?

Therefore Marcus, my brother in Christ, continue to love the scripture as you do. But do not be bound to the letter. The letter kills; the Spirit gives life.

Test what I have taught you

Examine all that I have said about women in my earlier letters and see if that is what the Spirit would require of us today. Would it please God or would it wound God's heart if all God's children were seen to be equal in God's sight?

Would God be displeased if all God's people, women and men, were to be prophets and priests setting forth the glory of God before all nations?

Would the message of the gospel be enhanced or diminished by permitting women to speak of the wonderful deeds God has done in their lives? Or should we suppress their witness to the power of the gospel because "Paul has ordained that women should not speak in the church"?

I am not pleased by those who presume to defend my teachings on the place of women in the church by insisting that everything I wrote about women and the family applies literally today. In no way do I consider them my allies in the gospel.

By defending word-for-word what I have written, they deny the tradition which is my own, in which the word once spoken must be made to speak again and again, through interpretation and adaptation, to new situations, so that it remains a living word.

Is there nothing permanent in scripture?

"How can this be?", some will ask. If what matters is the interpretation of the scripture, how does one discern the will of God? Would not every person have his or her own interpretation of the scripture? Is it not inviting danger to move away from the actual words of scripture?

Such fears are justified. However, do not believe those who want to convince you that it is therefore the letter which must be followed. I want you to be aware that the scripture has always been interpreted in context — by the Lord himself, by the apostles and throughout the history of the church.

Consider this. In response to the question, "What must I do to inherit eternal life?", Jesus told the rich young man that he should sell everything he had and give the money to the poor, and then follow our Lord (Matt. 19:16-22).

Do we say that this instruction is clear, and that all who want to have eternal life should sell everything they have and give the proceeds to the poor?

No. The very people who argue for the literal inspiration of scripture would say — not wanting to give up all their wealth — that Jesus said this to a rich young ruler and that it does not apply to them personally. They would insist on taking seriously the context in which Jesus spoke these words.

Why then should what I wrote to the women in Corinth or in a letter to Timothy become universally applicable to all women in all times? What of the specific context? What of the specific problems these churches were facing? What of the place of women in the society to which I was writing?

Would the word of God not become more clear if it was always understood in context and applied faithfully to the new context?

But I am aware that I have not yet dealt with the primary question of what is true interpretation.

Discerning the gospel

Let me say this. That which sets forth the glorious liberty of the gospel, builds on the firm foundation of the love of God revealed to us in Christ, upholds the community of faith and seeks to fulfill the true intentions of the gospel comes from the Spirit.

On the contrary, that which binds us into slavery, diminishes our humanity, disrupts community and comes from anything except love is not of the Spirit.

Therefore not all interpretations of scripture are correct; not all applications of scripture are of the Spirit. Learn to test the spirits, knowing that what does not give life is of the devil.

Quoting scripture by itself is of no avail. Even the devil quoted the scripture to tempt our Lord away from his obedience to God.

Search for scriptural support

You have also written that there does not seem to be sufficient scriptural support for the ordination of women, and that what the scripture does say seems to suggest that they should seek other forms of ministry in the church.

Although I have already written on this matter, here I would like to emphasize how scripture itself can provide the inspiration to go forward on such issues.

You recall how Peter was compelled by a vision to go to the house of the Roman centurion Cornelius (Acts 10). Now it was not the custom for a Jew to enter the home of a Gentile — certainly not to stay and eat there.

But Peter, having seen a vision in which he was asked not to consider unclean what God has made clean, found the courage not only to enter the Gentile home but also to confess to the Gentile audience that he now truly understood "that God shows no partiality, but in every nation anyone who fears him and does what is right is acceptable to him" (v.34).

Again, consider my own faith journey. You know how zealous I was for my own tradition; yet when I was gripped by the power of the gospel to break down barriers, I fought hard for the integration of the Gentiles into the life of the church. In so doing I was changing some of the accepted traditions that were also supported by the scriptures.

For doing so I was threatened, expelled, beaten up, thrown into prison. Several times my very life was in danger. But once I was clear in my own mind that it was by God's free gift of grace that all are saved, Jews and Greeks, I was willing to struggle with my own scripture and tradition, to reunderstand and restate it so as to make manifest the truth of the gospel.

Was I moving away from the traditions of our forebears? Was I acting in ways that seemed to stray from the teachings of the scriptures? Did I upset those who wanted to cling to the words of scripture?

Indeed. But I could not do otherwise, because I could not deny that through the death and resurrection of our Lord, God has made us into one people, and has equally bestowed on us the gifts of the Spirit.

Therefore, I ask those who wish to defend me to maintain not the words I have written but the gospel I preached. Do not defend my words that "man is the head of the woman", because here I was speaking at a period of time and out of a social context in which man was indeed seen as the head of the household. But defend my proclamation that in Christ there is "neither Jew nor Greek, slave nor free, male nor female", because this is the gospel.

But do not ask me when I was speaking as a man and when I was speaking as the announcer of the gospel. And do not say to me that you do not know when I speak in one way, and when in another.

If the gospel is written in your hearts, if the Spirit of God dwells in you, you know what is right and well-pleasing in God's sight.

Therefore, do not say, "The scriptures are the inspired word of God", for what does it profit you to say so? Do the scriptures need this attestation from you?

Rather, say to yourself, "The Spirit inspires me to find the word of God in the scriptures". Then you will not fall into the bondage of slavery to the written word, but will be free to be led by the Spirit to discern from the scriptures what God requires of you today.

The nature of inspiration

So if you are looking for inspiration in scripture, be inspired by the courage of Peter, who entered a Gentile home and thus upset a whole tradition because of a vision he was given.

Be inspired by the Council at Jerusalem (Acts 15) which, though made up entirely of Jewish Christians, sought a way for the church to become a truly universal fellowship in which Jews and Greeks and others would be one.

And be inspired by the way the Lord set me aside to be an apostle to the Gentiles, so that despite many trials and tribulations I was able to set forth the glorious message of the gospel that in Christ all barriers had been broken down.

Therefore, Marcus, my co-worker and beloved friend in the Lord, I ask you not to be shaken by those who quote scripture or argue from tradition to keep women under the domination of men and away from the ministry of the church.

It is the very same scripture which proclaims that we were created as male and female in the image of God; it is the same scripture which says that God shows no partiality and that all who believe are equal in God's eyes. It is the same scripture which proclaims that it is the death and resurrection of our Lord Jesus by which all of us have been saved and made into the one body.

The scriptures attest that each of us is called to be a witness, and that the Spirit of God bestows the gifts that are necessary for our ministries.

What more can I say? What more inspiration do you need from the scripture? To whom are you accountable besides the Spirit of God? What do you need to defend other than the truth that the church is truly the body of Christ?

I have no wish to overwhelm you with arguments or to prove anybody to be in the wrong. But I insist that those who are unwilling to discern where the Spirit of God is leading us and seek scriptural quotations to prevent such discernment have fallen back into slavery. They are of no help to you.

I advise you therefore to continue to help your congregation in the study of scripture and in the discernment of what it says to us today, so that together you may discover the will and purpose of God for all.

Closing greetings

Those who live with me send you warm greetings. Greet all my friends in your household with a holy kiss. And remember me in your prayers so that my love for the gospel and for the word of God which carries it may never falter.

May the peace of God fill your heart, and may the Spirit of God keep your heart and mind in the knowledge and love of our Lord Jesus Christ. And may glory, honour, praise and thanksgiving be to our God for ever and ever. Amen.